PR.

FOR

YOUTHS

AND

TEENAGERS

TELLA OLAYERI

Author of Fire for Fire

08023583168

Email; tellaolayeri@gmail.com

Website tellaolayeri.com.ng

APPRECIATION

I give special appreciation to my children and wife **MRS NGOZI OLAYERI** for her assistance in ensuring that this book is published. Also, this manuscript wouldn't have seen the light of the day, if not for the spiritual encouragement I gathered from my father in the Lord. **Dr. D. K: OUUKOYA** who served as spiritual mirror that brightens my hope to explore my calling (Evangelism).

We shall all reap our blessings in heaven but the battle to make heaven is not over, until it is won.

HELP OTHERS

No amount of money can buy divine help. It is good to teach others how to fish rather than give them fish. What I mean is it will be of great help if you buy one or two copies of this book as gifts for friends or neighbours. Many wants to pray but do not know how go about it. Thousands around you need your help. Give spiritual helping hands so that God may enlarge your coast as well. Do this today and God shall open the windows of heaven unto you, as you pray through this book.

PREVIOUS PUBLICATIONS OF THE AUTHOR

1. *Fire for Fire Prayer Book Part 1*

2. *Fire for Fire Prayer Book Part 2*

3. *Bye Bye to Poverty Part 1*

4. *Bye Bye to Poverty Part 2*

5. *My Marriage Shall Not Break*

6. *Prayer for Pregnant Women*

7. *Prayer for Fruit of the Womb*

8. *Children Deliverance*

9. *Prayer for Youths and Teenagers*

10. *Magnetic Prayer for Singles*

11. *Victory over satanic house Part 1*

12. *Victory over satanic house Part 2*

13. *I Shall Excel*

14. *Atomic Prayer Points*

15. *Goliath at the gate of marriage*

16. *Deliverance from Spirit of Dogs*

17. *Naked warriors*

18. *Power to Overcome Sex in the Dream*

19. *Strange Women! Leave My Husband Alone*

20. *Dangerous Prayer against Strange Women*

PREFACE

This prayer book is primarily written to teach and train youths and teenagers the act of spiritual warfare. Any child that wants to excel in spiritual warfare, academics, wisdom, physical needs and intercession cannot but do without having a copy of this book. THIS BOOK IS AN EYE OPENER TO GREATER HEIGHTS OF SUCCESS IN LIFE.

My sincere message to anyone that procures this book is that a new chapter of victory is open for him or her in heaven and on earth;

So I congratulate you for having yours today!

HOW TO USE THIS BOOK

This book should not be read like a literature book. It is a prayer book of power. What you need to do is to hold it, read with concentration and seriousness, and take to all instructions given in the book.

You are advised to go into seven days fasting and prayers with this book to enable you uproot, dismantle and destroy hindrances before you. Let your fasting start from 6: 0'clock in the morning and end by 6: 0' clock in the evening as well.

After this exercise, make sure you use this book continuously.

Table of Contents

CHAPTER 1

THANKSGIVING

O Lord, You are great, loving, and merciful. Your majesty is incomparable. How wonderful you .are on the throne. I glorify your name and thank you for not casting me away.

O Lord, you are an uncreated creator that created the universe with ease, the Being before all beings. The creator of all things, the Lilly of the valley, the Greater than the greatest, the Mightier than the mightiest. You are my Shepherd and my Lord. Everlasting Father, **"Yours o Lord, is the greatness and the power and the glory and the majesty and the splendor for everything in heaven and earth is yours" 1 Chronicles 29:11.** I thank you Lord and bow down before you.

O Lord, I thank you because you are the fountain of love, fountain of peace, fountain of glory, fountain of success, fountain of knowledge and wisdom fountain of breakthrough and fountain of salvation. You are the Lord of lords, and King of kings. I Am that I Am, the unchangeable God.

NOW SING:-
UNCHANGEABLE,
UNCHANGEABLE GOD
UNCHANGEABLE,
UNCHANGEABLE GOD
JEHOVAH NISSI
UNCHANGEABLE,
UNCHANGEABLE GOD
UNCHAGEABLE,
UNCHANGEABLE GOD.

I thank you Lord because during and. after this prayer enemies of my soul shall be chased out. By this prayer Lord, let my eyes see good things of life and my ears to hear good results.

O Lord, you are full of glamour, peace and joy. I thank you O Lord for your protection and loving kindness unto my family. I thank you O Lord for you shall turn the bitterness in my life to sweetness as in the order of bitter waters of Marah which became sweet before the Israelites in the desert of shur. I thank you Lord for keeping me alive and for restoring my soul.

Mountains and hills may crumble but God's love for me shall never fail. I thank you Lord for using your power to restore me unto you. For I shall dwell in the mountain of the Lord and in the sanctuary of His mercy. Amen.

FORGIVENESS OF SIN.

O Lord of mercy, have mercy on me. Let those who are against me without cause or against me due to omission or error have a change of mind towards me. Forgive me Lord, cancel every idle word I spoke or made against myself. O Lord forgive me sins I committed causing blockage, suffering, backwardness and unfulfiliment in me. I receive your forgiveness as I forgive those who sinned against me. **"Let the words of my mouth, and the meditation of my heart, be acceptable in thy sight, O Lord, my Strength, and my Redeemer". Psalm 19: 14.**

Host of heaven, take stock of my life and cancel shortcomings eroding my spiritual balance sheet. Reveal myself to me in the dream Lord, so that I may know my spiritual level. **"Look upon my affliction and my pain and forgive all my sin" psalm 25:18.**

I surrender by fire, whatever may disturb me from achieving my destiny. By this, I do away with my "Ishmael" (mistakes) and welcome my "Isaac" (success), in the name of Jesus. I renounce every form of gossip, bitter words, anger, fighting, un-forgiveness etc. that may give enemies opportunities to fire arrows against me.

(Touch your body and say this) My flesh I marry you to Christ this day. You shall not lead me to sin or be a hindrance to my salvation. For it is written **"Therefore, since Christ suffered in his body, arm yourselves also with the same attitude, because he who has suffered in his body is done with sin. As a result, he does not lie the rest of his earthly life for evil human desires, but rather for the will of God" 1 Peter 4:1-2.** Hence, as from today, I liberate my eyes, my mouth, my hands, my legs and heart from every form of sin in the name of Jesus. Amen.

O Lord forgive every sin committed by my parents forgive my family of ancestral sins of human sacrifice, Idolatry and witchcraft, Satan may use against us. We shall not bow before idols, evil altars, shrine or power of darkness any longer but for Christ our Saviour. For it is written, **"That at the name of Jesus, every knee should** bow in heaven and on earth and under the earth, and every tongue confess that Jesus Christ is Lord, to the glory of God the father" Philippians 2:10-11. Hence Lord, break down every one in my family from committing sin and destroy every wall of sin that surrounds us.

God of justice show me compassion. For it is written, "Blessed is he whose transgression is forgiven, whose sin is covered. Blessed is the man unto whom the LORD imputeth not iniquity, and in whose spirit there is no guile". Psalm32:1-2. My vision to serve you Lord shall not be thwarted by sins, nor shall my race and mission to make heaven fail. Amen.

COVER YOURSELF WITH BLOOD OF JESUS.

I cover my family and self, with blood of Jesus. I soak my life in the pool blood of Jesus and hold it as shield against satanic powers. I cover myself with blood of Jesus and claim access to the presence of the Lord Almighty. I attach my destiny unto God by the blood of Jesus.

I wash myself clean of evil marks and drink blood of Jesus as a baby drink's sweet syrup as energizer in today's battle. Blood of Jesus flush, redeem and purify me of inherited or self-acquired evil deposits; Blood of Jesus, heal me of evil growth and infirmity. Lord Jesus cleanse scars of sins and all forms of filthy garments In me by your blood. Wipe every disappointment, frustration and tragedies, spirit of anger, revenge and stubbornness wrecking my spiritual life. Let joy, love, goodness and peace occupy my mind,

By the power in your blood Lord, let me record outstanding victory and success over my enemies in this battle. For it is written, **"...they overcome him by the blood of the lamb and by the word**

of their testimony ....." Revelation 12:11. Let your blood separate me from powers of darkness. Blood of Jesus, separate me and my family from ancestral sins and unholy acts.

Blood of Jesus revive and resurrect good things that are dead in me. Refresh me anew this day O Lord with your fresh anointing to excel in life. Hence, I receive virtues, strength, power, might and special anointing from your precious blood.

I hold blood of Jesus against powers of stagnation. I hold it against evil diversion, failure at the edge of breakthrough and fruitless efforts in life. I hold it against powers of demotion, financial stagnation, business failure, career failure and academic failure. I hold it against dead account, failure to get helpers in time of need and against loss of foreign benefits. Hence, I pull down every stubborn mountain in my life, career and destiny in the name of Jesus.

EMPOWER YOURSELF WITH HOLY GHOST POWER.

My spirit receive Holy Ghost anointing. Fire of revival fall upon me for signs and wonders; perform spiritual sanitation in my life. Make my heart your temple; erase pollution that may hinder your stay in me.

O Lord incubate me with power and spirit to do your will. Holy Ghost Power, suppress mid destroy works of Satan in me. For **"...the Lord is the spirit, and where the spirit of the Lord is, there is freedom" 2Corinthians. 3:17.** Hence Lord increase yourself in me, incubate me with fire of righteousness that leads one to eternal life.

Fill my spirit with power and zeal to pray. Fill my soul with boldness and strength. Equip me with two-edged sword that will enable me fight my enemies and with divine gun that will silence my attackers: Anoint me with power no one can threaten. Hence, I shall not be second hand Christian or a push over in the camp of enemies. I shall wax stronger and stronger, while my enemies shall be weak and weaker, in the name of Jesus.

(POINT TO HEAVEN AND SAY) Thou evil clouds in the heavenly against my prayer disappear by fire in the name of Jesus. Every Satanic battle in the heavenly against my prayer receive defeat without delay in the name of Jesus. I reject every authority of wickedness over my destiny because the power of the Lord is upon me. Therefore my star shall arise and shine to proclaim the word of the Lord, in Jesus name I pray. Amen. (YOU CAN RELEASE YOUR HANDS).

I release fire of Holy Ghost into this environment, to destroy pillars and mountains that may stand as hindrance against my prayer life. My Lord shall make me his/her instrument of war against every form of powers of darkness and nullify evil authorities against my life. Hence, I arrest, detain and destroy every contrary power operating in this vicinity.

CHAPTER 2

PRAYER LADDER

My Lord and my God listen to my petition, answer my prayer, beside you I have no other person or power to help me. **"O keep my soul, and deliver me. Let me not be ashamed, for I put my trust in thee" Psalm 25:20.** Release your angels to fight this battle for me. Empower positive force within me to swallow every negative force battling with my life. At the end Lord convert my trials to testimonies, my scars to stars and my disappointment to appointments in Jesus name I pray. Amen.

I pray for divine fresh anointing, for the Lord **"……...giveth power to the faint, and to them that have no might he increaseth" Isaiah 40:29.** O Lord hear my prayer, give me peace as answer. Let your fear occupy my soul while my soul is filled with trust in you.

As I pray Lord, do not allow my prayer arrow miss its target. Let my prayer arrows cause confusion and civil war in the kingdom of Satan. Incubate me with divine power to locate, enter and retrieve my virtues in possession of enemies. Hence, I bind and paralyze every power charged to oversee me in the name of Jesus.

O Lord strengthen my faith to fight this battle. For it is written, **"For you are my strength and he will make my feet like hind's feet, and he will make me to walk upon my high places" Habakkuk 3:19.** One thing I know in this battle is, in the deepest depths my enemies shall be defeated, and in the highest heights they shall be losers.

(NOW HOLD YOUR HEAD WITH YOUR HAND AND PRAY LIKE THIS). As fish swim and make way in the waters with head and succeed, my head shall witness success and breakthrough in the name of Jesus. My head shall not answer evil call or evil summon in the day or at night in the name of Jesus. My head shall not be target of cutlass, axe attack or gun shots. My head shall, not reject gold for bronze or glory for shame in the name of Jesus. My head, you shall not reject upper class for lower class neither shall problems be your portion. Hence, I shall be the head and not the tail in the name of Jesus.

My head, you shall not disappoint me. Therefore, I cry unto you, arise and awake by fire in the name of Jesus! Live above evil arrows enemy may fire against you. My head, you shall not reject prayers neither shall you be target of insanity. You shall be seen and recognized anywhere you go. My head you are created for golden crown therefore receive it by fire in the name of Jesus. Henceforth, be a magnet of miracles, signs and wonders, in the name of Jesus. My head is not candidate of rod of darkness neither shall evil coconut be broken on it. My star shall rise and shine through you in Jesus name I pray.

Amen.

O Lord give me power to loose and bind as it is written in Isaiah 22:22, **"I will place on his shoulder the key to the house of David, what he opens no one can Shut and what he shuts no one can open".** Give me 'Lion heart' to move forward in my prayers. Make me a victorious warrior and conqueror over my enemies in the order of David versus Goliath. Let heavenly dizziness render my enemies helpless. Store reservoir of prayers in me to bombard and destroy powers of darkness until they shout loud like this in disgrace, **"Turn away from me: Let me weep bitterly. Do not try to console me ..." Isaiah 22:4**.

CHAPTER 3

PRAYER FOR FATHER.

O Lord empower my father to possess his possession and discharge his duties as the head of our home. My father, the Lord shall provide you to fulfill your role at home. You shall not fail nor fall as you fulfill your roles in the name of Jesus. Our Lord shall enlarge your coast to cater for our family. Amen.

The Lord Almighty shall guide you by pillar of fire by night and pillar of cloud by day before your enemies in the order of Israelites before the Egyptians. You shall not fail in any good step you take to better our lives.

The Lord shall be your shepherd and your guardian. My father, **"Arise shine, for thy light is come, and the glory of the Lord is risen upon**

thee" Isaiah 60:2B, Henceforth, enemies of your peace .shall receive divine slaps of madness.

My father you shall not die young, for it is written, **"Thy shoes shall be iron and brass, and as thy days, so shall thy strength be"** Every mission of the enemy against you shall not succeed but fall. Your stubborn pursuers shall perish in the Red Sea in the order of the Egyptians.

Cold arm of death shall not snuff life out of you. You shall not be candidate of hired assassins neither shall you be consumed in the valley or by the shadow of death.

O Lord dismantle and destroy every evil gate built around my father's success. My Lord and my God manifest and fulfill fruitfulness into his expectations. I command every evil seed and plantation growing in our home to wither and die. I reverse and render useless every negative decision taken against you by powers of darkness. By this, you shall not labour in vain but reap the fruit of your labour. Amen.

Thou power of resurrection bring life to the financial account of my father. As it is written, **"The rich rule over the poor, and the borrower is servant to the lender" Proverbs 22:7.** Therefore, my father you shall not be a borrower but lender to nations, in the name of Jesus. The treasures of the Lord shall open unto you. As you step out for your daily needs and activities; divine love peace, acceptance and adoration shall be your lot.

Heaven shall rain blessings and breakthroughs unto your life. Every contrary plan of the enemy to nail your success and career shall fail, in the name of Jesus.

Holy Ghost Power, destroy every power of darkness holding firm to the foundation of my father. Wicked aims of enemies against him shall not prosper. My father your enemies shall start their days in confusion and end it in disgrace. Holy Ghost, loose and free him from every form of bondage. My father (Mr. mention his name), it is written in the book of Isaiah 58: 11. **".......the Lord shall guide thee continually, and satisfy thy soul, in drought, and make fat thy bones and thou shalt be like a watered garden, and like a spring water, whose water fail not"**. This shall be your portion in the name of Jesus, Amen.

O Lord, let dryness and unfruitfulness be the portion of wicked powers running after my father. Let every wicked mirror used to control and monitor him break to pieces, in the name of Jesus. Any wicked arrow fired against him shall not prosper in the name of Jesus. My father, the Lord is assuring you this day saying, **"Do not fear, O Jacob my servant: do not be dismayed. O Israel. I will surely save you out of a distant**

place, your descendants from the land of their exile. Jacob will again have peace and security, and no one will make him afraid" Jeremiah 46:27.

Hence, any strongman delegated against you shall fail in the name of Jesus. Open disgrace shall be the portion of wicked powers assigned against you. The Lord Almighty shall empower you to stand against every evil force monitoring your life. As from today, your inner man shall not direct you wrongly, neither shall it confuse or fail you in the name of Jesus. Amen.

CHAPTER 4

PRAYER FOR MOTHER

O Lord spread your hand of love and protection upon my mother to fulfill her motherly role of caring, training and educate us rightly. Guide and protect my mother from threading on destructive paths of life. Holy Ghost, pull every evil lug in the eyes of my mother. Empower her to bring success and divine glory into our family. Give her wisdom to impact knowledge and understanding upon us, in the name of Jesus, Amen.

My mother, as from today the Lord shall make you hear from Him. The Lord shall open your eyes to see visions and open your ears to hear His divine calls. The Lord shall, fill your mouth with prayers and fill your heart with Power of revival. The Lord shall touch, remold and rename you as her daughter, in the name of Jesus

Hence, I rebuke spirit of 'Lot's wife' in your life and command· every, idol of your background aiming to pull you down to catch fire and roast to ashes, in the name of Jesus.

Cancer of the breast shall not be your portion neither shall milk that flows from it go sour or dry, in the name of Jesus. You shall not bury your children nor shall your children announce your premature obituary. Paralysis of the body, of legs and hands shall not be your portion. Your womb shall not obey evil call, obey evil command or experience arrow of unfruitfulness. As from today smiles shall fill your heart as it is written, **"A happy heart makes the face cheerful, but heartache crushes the spirit" Proverbs 15:13.**

Satan shall not turn you to his handbag or turn you adulterous. Any power that says you shall not prosper shall not have way in your life. You shall not be arrested by witchcraft powers nor be lured into it. Anyone that tries it shall fail in the name of Jesus. Hence, any power of darkness in your life shall not prosper but be punctured by the power of the Holy Ghost. Amen.

Nine months pregnancy and labour you pass through during child labour shall not be in vain. Satan shall not, double cross you from enjoying the fruits of your labour. You shall witness and taste the joy, success and peace of your children. By this, any power coming to attack you: shall fail. You shall not shed tears in respect of your children In the name of Jesus.

I command every Goliath raining curse at you or threatening your life to summersault and die. You shall move from victory to victory and experience success to breakthroughs. O Lord of mercy close and render useless every door of failure, every door of infertility, every door of infirmity, every door of sadness, every door of backwardness, every door of sorrow and every door of confusion fashioned against my mother. The love of God towards you shall not decrease, for it is written, **"For as high as the heavens are above the earth, so great is his love for those who fear him" Psalm 1 03:11.**

Every spirit of rag hunting your life shall die, while every power of darkness planting evil seeds in your life shall be roasted to ashes. Every work of darkness against your life shall be fruitless. I uproot and destroy every yoke of slavery and unfruitfulness upon your life. I command wall of fire to demarcate, you from all unfriendly friends in the name of Jesus.

My mother wherever you go, you shall **"find favour and good understanding in the sight of God and man" Proverbs 3:4**. Every trap of enemy against you shall fail. No weapon fashioned against you shall prosper while every arrow of darkness fired against you shall go back to senders and consume them. The Lord shall empower you above every hardship in life in Jesus name I pray. Amen.

CHAPTER 5

PRAYER FOR FAMILY /NEIGHBOURS

O Lord save my family from destruction, **"blotting out the handwritings or ordinances that was against us and which was contrary to us" Colossians 2:14A.** Your encouragement and support shall be the source of our strength, Thou evil anointing of disunity in my family dry up in the name of Jesus. My family, unity shall reign among us in the order of Jesus and His disciple. Any spirit of Judas Iscariot (spirit of betrayal) that may rear its ugly head among us shall die in the name of Jesus. I bind and destroy every spirit of Ananias and Saphira that may bring abrupt end to our family lineage. I bind every spirit of Gehazi that may bring disgrace into our family in the name of Jesus.

O Lord empower my family to abide in you, provide, for us our daily bread. I cancel evil effects

.of ancestral names and dedications affecting the moving forward of our family. My family shall not eat food of idleness nor feed in frustration. No tough time shall make us bow to Satan in the name of Jesus. For we shall serve the Lord, **"Who hath translated us into the .Kingdom of his dear Son" Colossians: 13**. The faith of my family to you Lord shall not be eroded by evil powers.

Thou power of darkness challenging the destiny of my brothers and sisters be nullified in the name of Jesus. Holy Ghost destroy every power; giving strength to enemies of my family, I file divine counter report against evil reports eroding our lives. O Lord guide and distance every member of my family from powers pursuing them day and night, by pillar of cloud by day and pillar of fire by night, in the order of Israelites before the Egyptians.

God of Elijah consume by fire evil files that has my family names for attack and destruction. Hence, any power that troubles the Israel of my family shall be troubled by the God of Elijah in the name of Jesus. Thou power of darkness behind our cause know one thing today **"it is not by sword or spear that the Lord saves; for the battle is the LORD'S and He will give all of you unto our hands"** 1 Samuel 17:47. Hence, I command every Power in charge of evil altars in my family to die, for the Lord shall be our shepherd and we shall not want. Amen.

O Lord provide for everyone in my family and neighbours divine instrument of victory, divine instrument of testimonies, divine instrument of excellence and divine instrument of breakthroughs proclaim your name as our Lord and Saviour. Enlarge the coast of my neighbours and family members' multiply our resources beyond human imagination:

Host of heaven support, fight against every contrary power holding us captive. Lord Jesus overturn tables of poverty set before us, never allow us beg for bread.

O Lord save my family and neighbours from every form of oppression, terror and depression of mind. Holy Ghost frustrate efforts of territorial spirits working against my neighbor and my household. Let scarcity be a thing of past in our lives.

Thou satanic ladder used to gain entrance into our lives break in the name of Jesus. In joint efforts, we close every wicked access of hell fire into our lives. Hence Lord, nullify every evil yoke and ordination shouldered by us. Though, **"Some trust in chariots, and some in horses: but we will remember the name of the LORD our God"**.

Holy Ghost, uproot and destroy every seed of poverty and evil plantation growing in the garden of our lives.

Lift from us evil loads placed upon our shoulders. O Lord **"Deliver my soul from the sword; my darling from the power of the dog" Psalm 21:20** By this, let every arrow of destruction fired against us, go back to the sender and consume them, in the name of Jesus. Amen.

CHAPTER 6

PRAYER FOR MEN OF GOD

The Holy Bible says, **"Pray for the peace of Jerusalem: they shall prosper that love thee. Peace be within thy walls, and prosperity within thy palaces" Psalm 122:6-7**. Hence I pray for the peace of my nation and men of God at large. O Lord cover my General Overseer (mention his name), my Pastor (mention his name) and Ministers of God with your precious blood. Envelop them with divine fire. Incubate them with leadership styles that will strength the church against any form of satanic advances. They are the shepherds while we are the flocks. By this, guide them against satanic attacks for if the shepherd is struck, the flock will scatter. Hence I pronounce wisdom, knowledge and understanding into their lives.

O Lord baptize them with powers of signs and wonders to prove you are the Lord. Let the sermons they preach bring faith and belief unto members. Let their teachings wake unbelievers and members from slumber. Open the ears of members for understanding and their eyes for visions.

The banner of the Lord shall not depart from them whatever they bind shall remain bound and whatever they lose shall remain loosed; In the name of Jesus They shall be elevated to the point where they shall be powers that pursue and not one pursued by enemies. They shall be tested and trusted soldiers of the Lord and shall by no means be defeated in the battle of life.

I nullify every verdict of enemies against them. Every instrument of destruction put in place against them shall not stand but fail. As from today, any power that try to frustrate them shall be frustrated and anyone that tries to disgrace them shall be disgraced. Every anti- Levi arrows fired against them shall not see the light of the day. No arrow of defeat or death shall prevail against them. Amen.

I command working angels of God to rise and fight their battles in the name of Jesus. The Lord shall visit their full time and part time enemies with vengeance, terror, anger, wrath, problems and hatred in the name of Jesus. Every Goliath of their lives shall meet failure. They shall triumph over their enemies seven fold in the name of Jesus.

O Lord hearken to my prayers on behalf of my General overseers, my pastors and ministers, in Jesus name I pray. Amen.

CHAPTER 7

PRAYER FOR WISDOM AND EXCELLENCE

O Lord, baptize me with knowledge and wisdom that will turn me to master in my career. Give me information that will positively improve me. Give me skills that will elevate me and good understanding that will enhance me before people. Give me understanding to know my goal and knowledge to achieve it, for a goalless youth is like a traveler without destination. By this, give me power and ability to do right thing at the right time, in the right way and at the right place. At the end Lord, give me wisdom to accomplish all round success in my endeavors. Amen.

I shall not experience fruitless labour in .my career. Hence, every hindrance against my academics like mind wandering during lecture time, day dreaming and lack of interest in my studies shall vanish in the name of Jesus. Holy Spirit remind me when to speak and when to be silent on issues. My stars arise and shine, refuse demonic burial, refuse to be darkened by power of darkness. I shall be the head and not the tail, I shall be above only and not beneath.

My prospects shall not be forfeited, my opportunities shall not die, and my talents shall not be wasted, in the name of Jesus. O God of signs and wonders crown me with your glory. Let testimonies of breakthrough overtake my destiny. Let my life be loaded with smiles and joy in the name of Jesus.

O Lord saturate my life with divine favour. Let doors of favour, windows of favour, gate of favour, open unto my life in the name of Jesus. From the north I shall be favoured, from the south I shall be favoured, from the east I shall be favoured, and from the west I shall be favoured in the name of Jesus. My boat of success shall not capsize; neither shall it be swallowed by forces of darkness. At the end of this prayer I shall be a winner in the name of Jesus. Amen.

Spirit of the living God come and place shield of protection around me. Thou spirit of bewitchment die and resurrect no more. Thou host of heaven arise, uproot and destroy every Goliath threatening my destiny. Thou enemy of my greatness be frustrated to shame in the name of Jesus. .

Holy Spirit, teach and incubate me with anointing of success that improves wisdom, knowledge and understanding. Inject me with supernatural tonic to excel and progress in life. Make me a yielding vessel for your work so that my life could bring praise and honour, unto you. O Lord let your goodness locate me and let my efforts be fruitful,

Make me a champion O Lord and let my usefulness be felt in my family and environ.

O Lord, you are the source of my joy and breakthrough, do not let me be used as rag or tissue paper in the hands of my enemies. Hence, baptize me with spirit of wisdom, spirit of revelation, spirit of enlightenment and, spirit of knowledge. My Lord and my God instruct, teach and guide me for excellence. For it is written,**"I will instruct thee and teach thee in the way, which thou shalt go: I will guide thee with mine eye". Psalm 32**:8. Thou powers of confusion running after me, whenever you turn left you shall meet disappointment, whenever you turn right you shall meet failure, whenever you turn front or back disgrace shall be your portion in the name of Jesus.

Revive me O Lord, illuminate me with divine light. I shall walk before you with righteousness for **"The light of the righteous rejoiceth! But the lamp of the wicked shall be put out". Proverbs 13:9.** O Lord disgrace my enemies, for pride is their; necklace, their cloth is, violence, while their speech, is full of malice. Last warning! Thou enemies of my soul my God warns you to desist from evil, for it is written, **"Take your evil deeds out of my sight! Stop doing wrong, learn to do right! Isaiah 1:16-17.**

CHAPTER 8

PRAYER WHILE IN SCHOOL OR AT

HOME.

O Lord, let my prayers shake and cause disaster in the kingdom of Satan. I contend with and defeat every hostility and attacks against my prayer life. Holy Ghost power incubate my prayer with fire, turn it to divine spiritual insecticide, spiritual virus killer and destroyer of every form of contrary powers that surrounds me for evil. You heavenly host, empower me to challenge the ground, challenge the sea, challenge rivers, challenge air, challenge the sun, moon and star against evil baptism of my academics, breakthrough, career and calling in the name of Jesus.

God of Elijah, fire arrow, throw hailstones, apply coals of fire, send lighting and thunder to scatter and destroy evil gatherings and forces against my soul Henceforth,- baptize me with spiritual power that will make me a hero in this battle.

Holy spirit divine, give me spirit of assimilation and concentration in the class, give me spirit to assess assignments rightly and spirit to assess myself rightly. In the presence of those asking me, "Where is your God"?, arise and prove yourself before them. Hence, I pronounce this special announcement- Thou cry of sorrow cry of tragedy and confusion meant for this year, my life is not your candidate. I shall be what God wants me to be and shall arise and shine above every other star that competes with me. Father Lord, increase my greatness, comfort, love, peace and prosperity. Abort every pregnancy of confusion and failure assigned against my academics in the name of Jesus.

Fire of God protect my star for good. Let walls and pillars of darkness erected against me collapse and scatter in the name of Jesus. Thou power of darkness assigned to pull me down be nullified by the blood of Jesus. My enemies listen and hear me well, "as food cures hunger and study cures ignorance" I shall graduate, secure good job and live an exemplary life in the name of Jesus.

O Lord, you are the 'Rock of Ages' turn me to rock enemies cannot contend with. Let all contrary powers that collide with me scatter and let anyone that contend with me for evil fail. Build and guide me spiritually, so that my physical struggle shall not be in vain. With this, no storm shall swallow me, no wind shall paralyze me, no river or flood shall sweep me away in the name of Jesus. No lightning or thunder of enemies shall consume me, no evil rain shall soak me; no power of the sun or power of the moon shall smite me in the name of Jesus.

O Lord empower me to fulfill my destiny frustrate works of emptier against me.

Holy Ghost Power, break every control and, links between earthly and heavenly demons against my life. Evil monitors of my life go blind forever. I break all curses and take authority over every cage of darkness that brings unhappiness into my life. I reject spirit of death and poverty hunting my life. By this Lord, place divine embargo against every harm and hurt of tongue, limiting my life.

O Lord reveal yourself, speak to me in the dream and in visions. Let your power of majesty scatter hopes of my enemies. Give me open victory before my detractors and let smiles of victory radiate in my face. Thou evil pot delegated against me in the dream break and scatter into pieces. Thou masquerade pursuing me in the dream summersault and die. Thou spirit spouse harassing me for sex in the dream die. Thou evil barber assigned to shave my hair in the dream in other to cut my glory short die in the name of Jesus. Thou powers of satanic alliance against my career and destiny scatter, in the name of Jesus.

The pit enemies dug for me shall swallow them, for it is, written, **"They will fall and be broken, they will be snared and captured" Isaiah 8:15**. By this their aims to destroy me shall fail in the name of Jesus. O Lord let your consuming, fire, devour every wicked power assigned against me, **"Let me not be ashamed O Lord, for I have called upon thee: let the wicked be ashamed, and let them be silent in the grave. Psalm 31:17.**

O Lord shake the foundations of my enemies and scatter their gathering. Render useless and ineffective any power assigned to reap the fruit of my labour. I refuse to labour and work like an elephant only to eat like an ant. Increase me O Lord in all my undertakings, **"……..increase my greatness and comfort me on every side"** **Psalm 71:21.**

Thou power of darkness terrifying me with fear die. O Lord paralyze efforts of the enemy that wants to envelope my life, my career and academics with frustration, failure and disappointment Deliver **"…...me from my strong enemy and from them, which hated me: for they were too strong for me" Psalm 18:17.** Storm of life shall not swallow me neither shall emptiness be my portion, Satisfaction of my enemies shall not sour **"as when a hungry man dreams that he is eating but he awakens and his hunger remains, as when a thirsty man dreams that he is drinking, but he awakens faint, with his thirst unquenched".**

O Lord let wailing and lamentation be the portion of my enemies. Let the blood of my enemies become fuel for fire that consumes them. Let their boasts turn empty, let their pride lead to self-defeat, .let their glory fade, let their homes turn to heap of ruins; let their plans turn to nothing.

(NOW POINT YOUR FINGER UNTO GROUND AND PRAY LIKE THIS) O ground open and swallow evil powers assigned against me. Hence, swallow poverty in my lineage, swallow sorrow and affliction troubling my life, swallow failure at the edge of breakthrough, and swallow strong man and strong woman pursuing me for evil. Power of nakedness shall not prosper in my life neither shall it prosper in my destiny. Thou ground which I am standing rebel not against me. Thou contrary powers that gather round my star in order to destroy or pull me down, enter the ground and die in the name of Jesus.

(NOW PRAY ON)

Every satanic move to render me useless in life scatter to pieces in the name of Jesus. Every cycle of poverty in my family line break. Every witchcraft arrow fired against me while I was in my mother's womb be rendered useless. O Heavenly Court, cancel and nullify warrant of arrest issue against me.

I cause every evil material magnetizing failure and defeat into my life to die. By the power of the living God, I restore good things which powers of emptier took away from me. Thou sun, moon, stars, earth, water, seas and oceans holding on to my possessions release them now in the name of Jesus.

As from today, enemies of my progress shall dwell in failure as my joy shall make them experience sorrow, my success shall lead to their failure, and my progress shall lead to their backwardness, while my financial breakthrough shall cause them to drown in penury.

At the end of this prayer, I shall harvest baskets of joy, basket of breakthrough and basket of academic excellence. I claim freedom from spirit of desolation, and every bondage and marks that wreck destiny. O Lord, let my brain flow with current of excellence and let powers that ruin destiny be far from me.

CHAPTER 9

PRAYER DURING EXAMINATION

O Lord of mercy rescue my mind from blankness, give me secrets to score high marks and grades in examinations. Bless my brain, give me knowledge and understanding to listen, study, read and memorize to excel in my academics. Errors and mistakes shall not be my lot during and after examinations, Power of failure shall not slaughter my career, neither shall it slaughter my destiny and happiness, in the name of Jesus. Hence, I declare power of excellence to flow in my life.

O Lord nullify spirit of procrastination, and spirit of fear and failure in my life. I command every spirit of destruction, every spirit of diversion, and every spirit of frustration fashioned against me to lose their hold and die in the name of Jesus. The fountain of my thoughts shall not dry while springs of fortunes to excel in life shall be my lot day and night in the name of Jesus.

Holy Ghost set me free from every form of defeat and failure targeted against me. Hence, I reject spirit of defeat, spirit of failure, spirit of error, spirit of stagnancy and every spirit of demotion fashioned against my academics, in the name of Jesus. I shall not fail but pass with flying colours in my examinations and I shall give all glory to the Lord Almighty. As enemies plan their evil acts so shall their plans be exposed in the name of Jesus.

My head, failure and loss of memory shall not be your portion. Every thought of good things that emanate from you shall lead me to success in life. Do not allow my legs walk into captivity Never allow my mind be captivated for evil, or allow my mouth lead me to trouble as all thoughts emanates from the head.

Thunder fire of God break into pieces every evil pot used to summon my life in the spirit. Holy Ghost Power break and destroy any carved image used by enemies to regulate and control my life for failure. Hence, I paralyze every negative dream meant to pollute my life and destiny.

I bind, neutralize and destroy every source of power and energy drawn from the air, drawn from the wind, drawn from fire, drawn from water, sea or ocean, drawn from the sun, the moon and the star to bring failure into my academics, career or life in the name of Jesus. By this, I shall not fail nor die in the course of my study. For it is written of me in Isaiah 43:2, **"When thou passest through the waters, I will be with thee, and through the rivers, they shall not overflow thee: when though walkest through the fire, thou shalt not be burned, either shall the flame kindle upon thee"**

Every verdict of Witchcraft power against my career and calling scatter, in the name of Jesus. My destiny refuse sudden burial, refuse partial burial, refuse satanic burial, in the name of Jesus. I break every mechanism of automatic failure fashioned against my studies. By this all counsels of the enemy to thwart my academics shall fail, in the name of Jesus

O Lord turn my mourning to dancing, put off my sackcloth and guide me with gladness. **"Pull me out of the net that they have laid privately for me: for thou art my strength" Psalm 31:4.** By this, let no king or queen of darkness oversee my performance anymore, nor shall I be answerable to evil summons in the name of Jesus. My heaven open and rain surprises, luck and testimonies upon my destiny now and forever more, in the name of Jesus.

CHAPTER 10

PRAYER AGAISNT ACADEMIC KILLERS

O Lord hearken to my voice and answer me quickly because my power lies on prayers. **"Be not far from me, for trouble is near: for there is no one to help" Psalm 21:11**. Holy Ghost, kill spirit of fear holding me captive. Let my spirit eyes receive power; let my soul be free from every form of bondage and wickedness. Lord Jesus, you are a mighty man of war, great in battle, fight this battle for me.

NOW SING THIS SONG TWICE AND PRAY
You are the mighty man in battle Jehovah
You .are the mighty man in battle
Blessed be thy name.

O Lord nullify every wicked step taken by enemies against my life. Let every contrary spirit fashioned against me die. Thou star hijackers struggling with my star meet double failure today.

Thou power of God blow away every problem that surrounds me as chaff is blown by strong wind in the name of Jesus.

Thou angles of the living God draw your sword of defeat and axe of destruction in my defense against all powers that rise up against-me. I bind all dark powers with hot fetters of chain of God never to rise again. Holy Ghost, slaughter them without mercy, arrow of God strike them down. Let every giant standing at the gate of my breakthrough die in the name of Jesus. By this Lord, set me free from the hands of destiny killers and devourers of success.

Thou stubborn pursuers of my life I overcome you by Spirit of God. I command powers of Pharaoh in my life saying, "I shall not let you go" to die: My enemies shall meet failure and be crowned with crown of shame

My enemies shall be seated in the seat of disgrace, in the name of Jesus. By this every Goliath boasting against me saying "I shall enslave and destroy your destiny" shall die. Every power of Herod pointing finger of death at me saying "I shall kill you and your destiny at infancy" shall die, in the name of Jesus.

O Lord, reverse roaring waves and storms advancing against me. Let your burning anger consume my enemies by fire. O Lord, let ground and heaven carry out judgment in my favour. Hence, I fire back every satanic arrow fired against my destiny.

Thou evil power reluctant from leaving me alone, be disgraced out of my life. Thou evil horn scattering my hopes and virtues break, in the name of Jesus. Thou blood sucking demons delegated against me, get drunk with your, own blood and die. For it is written, **"And I will feed them that oppress thee with their own flesh, and they shall be drunken with their own blood as with sweet wine: and all flesh shall know that I the LORD am the Saviour and thy Redeemer, the mighty one of Jacob" Isaiah 49:26**. Hence 1 command every garment of failure, every garment of sorrow and every garment of shame designed for me to catch fire and roast to ashes, in the name of Jesus.

My life escape from the grip of powers of wasters delegated against me. Thou wasters in my foundation die. Thou spirit of waster delegated against my life die. I say wasters! wasters!, wasters! in my life, die, die, die in the name of Jesus: 1 gain my freedom by fire. Your battle shall not prevail against me in the name of Jesus.

I shall not lament in sorrow neither will I be a candidate of slaughter house in the hands of money makers. By this, my life shall not be wasted, my talent shall not be wasted, my energy shall not be wasted, and my destiny shall not be wasted, in the name of Jesus. I recover every good thing which powers of wasters stole from me seven fold in the name of Jesus. I paralyze and destroy powers of wasters in my life and receive total deliverance in Jesus name. Henceforth, any power that refuses to let me go but keep on pursuing me shall run mad and die. For it is written **"I will make your enemies turn their backs and run" Exodus 23:27B.**

Deliver me 0 Lord from the snare of the fowler, from the noisome pestilence of the wicked. Save me from being overtaken or over powered by wicked forces of the day or of the night. For it is written, **"Thou shalt not be afraid for the terror by night, nor for the arrow that flieth by day; nor for the pestilence that walketh in darkness, nor for the destruction that wasteth at noonday: A thousand shall fall at thy side,** and ten thousand at thy right hand, but it shall not come nigh thee" says the LORD Amen. Psalm 91:5-7.

CHAPTER 11

PRAYER AGAINST WICKED FORCES

(POINT AT THE HEAVENLY AS YOU PRAY THIS PARAGRAPH)

You my heaven co-operate with me, co-operate with my destiny, co-operate with my studies, co-operate with my career, co-operate with my talents, co-operated with my present and future, so that I may excel in life, in the name of Jesus.

Thou sun, thou moon, thou stars, thou cloud in the heavenly you shall not work against me. Every wicked decision taken by council of elders against me in the, heavenlies shall not prevail in the name of Jesus. In this prayer Lord, let the actions of detractors against me fail. Let their works destroy them and let their breath become gas and fire that destroy them. O Lord, give quick answer to my prayer. Let me experience immediate miracles to my petitions and let signs and wonders overshadow my situation, in the name of Jesus.

(NOW SHAKE YOUR BODY AS YOU PRAY THIS PRAYER)

Afflictions, afflictions, afflictions in my life come out by fire and die. Every bondage in my life be purged by blood of Jesus. Thou witchcraft sickness and diseases enemies fired against me I shake you off by fire. I shake away every infirmity in my body. I shake away poverty in my life. I shake away sorrow and backwardness in my life. I shake away failure at the edge of breakthrough in the name of Jesus.

(NOW READ AND PRAY WITHOUT SHAKING YOUR BODY AGAIN)

Holy Ghost Power destroy the foundation, the backbone and the jaws of powers assigned against me. I send destructive lightning thunder of God into the camps of powers struggling with my star.

Thou house of darkness where my destiny is discussed for evil catch fire in the name of Jesus. Holy Ghost, smite the cheekbone of my enemies, break their teeth and dash them to pieces. May destructive flood, storm and tempest of God paralyze and destroy their existence in the name of Jesus.

Thou power of darkness competing with my testimony be disgraced. Thou spirit of waster delegated against my destiny be buried alive. Thou power of the grave pursuing my life be silenced. Thou serpent of darkness in my life die in the name of Jesus. For it is written, **"The Lord shall cause thine enemies that rise up against thee to be smitten before thy face: They shall come against thee one way; and flee before thee seven ways" Deuteronomy: 28:7.**

My father, my father, release me speedily from powers of witchcraft. I command any power assigned to abort my academics and career to die. I command powers manipulating my life to scatter by fire. Divine power of God swallow serpents of darkness delegated against me in the order of Moses before Pharaoh. I command every wickedness of the wicked against me to stop by fire for glory of God to shine upon me. No power of darkness shall swallow me for it is written, **"Thy (my enemies) are brought down and fallen: But we (I and my family) are risen, and stand upright" Psalm20:8.**

O Lord save me from eating in the dream, from being oppressed in the dream, from evil pursuit in the dream and from every form of marine spirit and arrest in the dream. O Lord cancel every evil dream enemies use to choke my life. My spirit, soul and body refuse to cooperate with witchcraft influence. Thou power assigned to make love with me in the dream die shatter to pieces.

Lord confront, confuse, disgrace, defeat and destroy every witchcraft power, sorcerer, and any form of adversity of the enemy against my life. Thou host of heaven raise double standard of war against my enemies, make them experience double destruction and defeat. My enemies, **"Thy terribleness hath deceived thee, and the pride of thine heart, O thou that dwellest in the clefts of the rock, that holdest the height of the hill: though thou shouldest make thy nest as high as eagle, I will bring thee down from thence, said the LORD" Jeremiah 49:16.** My enemies, be trapped in your traps, be blind folded by the lightning of God, be consumed by unquenchable fire of God and be arrested by the fear of the day and the fear of the night. May your forces be defeated by angelic force of God. At last thou shall experience sudden burial.

I shoot stones of fire to scatter and dismantle thrones of witchcraft fashioned against me. I command owners of evil load in my life to carry their loads by fire in the name of Jesus. Holy Ghost Fire, destroy evil luggage of destruction enemies have for me in the name of Jesus. God of Elijah roast to ashes every altar of witchcraft, every foundation of witchcraft, every refuge and secret places of witchcraft hunting my life. May the scattering whirlwind of God decamp and destroy their existence, in the name of Jesus.

O Lord my God don't fold your, arms until you complete your rescue in respect of my life. Hence, convert my opposition to acceptance, convert my weakness to strength, convert my fear to assurance convert my sorrow to fullness of joy, convert my plans to action, convert confusion in me to settlement of mind and convert your promises for me to fulfillment, in Jesus name I pray. Amen.

CHAPTER 12

PRAYER WHEN TRAVELLING

O Lord in every journey I partake, save my life, save my property, save my career, and destiny from every form of destruction. Any power saying I shall be consumed on my way shall experience disappointment, disgrace and failure in the name of Jesus. In my journey, I shall not witness accident on my way neither shall I experience untimely death, in the name of Jesus. Anyone that set evil trap for me shall fall into it while any power warming up to suck my blood shall suck his or her own blood. By this Lord, **"Let them be confounded and put to shame that seek after my soul: let them be turned back and brought to confusion that devise my hurt" Psalm 35:4.**

Holy Ghost destroy every contrary power delegated against me in the firmament, in the air, in the sun, in the moon and in the star to monitor my journey for evil.

Hence, I pronounce judgment of death upon every witchcraft power, marine power, demons and every wicked power assigned against me. I cancel my name from satanic registers, list of accident victims and candidates for emergency or mass burial, in the name of Jesus. My soul stay far from destruction and terminal death. For it is written, **"The Lord redeemeth the soul of his servants: and none of them that trust in him shall be desolate" Psalm34:22**. O Lord of glory disgrace every effort of enemies against my career.

O Lord bring the counsel of the wicked to naught and their devices to no effect. Thou power of God, melt and destroy my materials and personal belongings held in the altar of darkness. Thou wicked altar waiting to celebrate with my blood your time is up die, in the name of Jesus. Thou spirit of untimely death and power of coffin assigned against me in the spirit catch fire and roast to ashes in the name of Jesus. Thou wicked magnet calling my soul and spirit to slaughter house of darkness for destruction catch fire and burn to ashes.

I shall not set on journey of no return, for the Lord said unto me, **"Behold I give unto you power to tread on serpents and scorpions, and over all the power of the enemy: and nothing shall by any means hurt you" Luke 10:19.** Thus, as night gives way for morning, and morning gives way for afternoon so shall my enemies give way for my safety. By this, I bind every contrary spirit and power that may monitor me, lead me astray or shoot wicked arrows against me in the name of Jesus. My God shall render them useless day in day out from causing me sorrow.

CHAPTER 13

PRAYER FOR GOOD HEALTH

O Lord my God, guide and protect me for you are the Lion of the tribe of Judah powers of darkness cannot withstand or suppress. O Lord guide me against eating what will eventually destroy me or drink what will kill me. O Lord do not allow my enemies pour me out like wasted water, or allow my bones be out of my joints, nor my heart melt like wax. Guide me with your fire of protection so that **"when evil men advance against me to devour my flesh, when my enemies and my foes attack me they will stumble and fall" Psalm 27:2.**

Thou power of God, suffocate and destroy every contrary power on evil assignment to inject me with sickness and destructive virus. **"Yea, though I walk through the valley of the shadow of death, I will fear no evil: for thou art with me,**

thy rod and thy, staff they comfort me" Psalm
23:4.

O Lord disband all hosts of sickness and diseases
in my life. O Lord of mercy heal me of every
infirmity and sickness; and of afflictions and
diseases in my life touch me with your hand of
healing, strengthen and destroy every symptom of
sickness and diseases in my life. By your power
Lord, cancel all problems programmed into my
life through dream and conspiracy of the wicked.
By this, ill health, sickness, disease, insanity and
untimely death shall not be my portion, in the
name of Jesus.

O Lord open my ears with your divine key of
liberation to hear and recognize your voice.
Occupy my heart to enable me obey you in
totality. For it is written **"If you listen carefully
to the voice of the Lord your God and do what
is right in his eyes,....I will not bring on you**

any of the diseases I brought on the Egyptians" Therefore, O Lord save my purse and resources from leakages, keep my family from bankruptcy which sickness may cost us. Hence Lord, nullify every form of satanic power against me, give me divine health and vitality. For it is written, **"Then shall thy light break-forth as the morning, and thine health shall spring forth speedily: and thy righteousness shall go before thee the-glory of the Lord shall be thy reward" Isaiah 58:8**

I shall not live a sorrowful life, live a confused life nor be contented with life in the valley. I break and loose myself from every covenant of failure and sickness in the name of Jesus. I break every evil covenant and evil initiation linking me with any power of darkness. As from today, sickness shall not be my portion neither shall storm of disease send me to untimely grave. I cleanse every dust of death in my life and drink blood of Jesus to purify my system in Jesus name I pray. Amen.

I dismantle every evil altar and evil shrine fashioned against me. I nullify every destructive incantation and spell issued against me. For it is written **"There shall no evil befall thee neither shall any plague come nigh thy dwelling" Psalm 91:10**. Holy Ghost Power dethrone every evil spirit reigning in my life. Strangers of darkness in my body come out by fire and die. Every negative scan reports awaiting maturity in my life be cancelled in the name of Jesus. Thou evil hand assigned to push me into destruction, wither by fire. Thou evil eye firing wicked arrows against me, go blind forever in the name of Jesus. Thou blood sucking power delegated against me die. Thou satanic animals assigned to harm me die in the name of Jesus. By this Lord, baptize my enemies with sudden terror and wasting diseases.

Thou power of darkness, no matter where you hide, come out by fire and receive divine judgment of destruction. Thou plantation of darkness in my destiny, what are you waiting for? wither and die in the name of Jesus. Thou evil deposit planted in my life in the dream die and rise no more. Thou arrow of sickness and disease fired against my life back fire by fire in the name of Jesus. Save me Lord from evil arrows but send wasting arrows against powers of darkness delegated against me. By this, any power firing arrow of sickness against me shall meet double failure while dangers ahead of me shall disappear by fire.

I command suckers of blood and eaters of flesh delegated against me to suck their own blood and eat their own flesh. I halt and destroy every work of witch doctor in my life. Let my enemies waste away like a terribly sick man hit by arrow of God. O Lord raise your staff over trouble waters of my life and dry it by fire. I thank you O Lord that you are bigger than my problems. "**O Lord my God, I cried unto thee, and thou hast healed me**" **Psalm 30:2** Thank you Jesus. Amen

CHAPTER 14

PRAYER FOR GOOD JOB AND SUCCESS IN

LIFE

My star arise and shine for your days of glory is, at hand. It is written, **"A star will come out of Jacob, a scepter will rise out of Israel"** **Numbers 24:17.** My star, you shall not be covered by darkness, nor be hidden or destroyed, in the name of Jesus. My star shall not dwell in the valley of failure but shall attain greater height and glory. Amen.

Thou evil padlock fashioned against me break and lose your hold, in the name of Jesus. O Lord let any man or woman ordained to help me, locate me and gallantly lift me up out of the pit of unemployment and stagnancy. O Lord, give me the spirit that do things rightly, that is, spirit that does not place the cat before the horse, nor sleep a sleep of failure. I shall not lack for **"The earth is the LORD'S and fullness thereof: the world and they that dwell therein"** **Psalm24:1.**

Because your resources are unlimited and because you do not know failure I shall win my crusade against unemployment.

O Lord let anointing that yield money and, cause financial breakthrough fall upon me. O Lord let miracles and blessings that have not taken place in my family line locate me by fire. You that return the captivity of Zion, return all I lost till date. Overshadow my life with divine miracles of the Lord. Make me bankers to my family and helpers to nations. Hence I draw bloodline of Jesus around my properties and possessions in the name of Jesus.

I refuse and reject any power threatening to imprison my destiny, my career, my life and household. **"Though the young lions do lack, and suffer hunger: but they that seek the LORD shall not want any good thing" Psalm 34:10.** On this planet earth, I shall pluck seeds of success and be a great achiever in the name of Jesus. Let the power of authority to excel fall upon me. Let your favour and good luck be my portion in the order of the woman with issues of blood whose faith find favour, good luck and miracle before, our Lord Jesus Christ.

Holy Ghost reveal and expose every hidden agenda of the enemy against my moving forward in life. Every satanic journalist spreading evil reports against me for failure at each junction of my life shall be overpowered by insanity. The race of enemy against me shall not succeed but fail for the Lord shall keep me abreast of them. Their strength shall fail them and shall by no means overtake or overpower me in the battle of life. **"An horse is a vain thing for safety: neither shall he deliver any by his great strength" Psalm 33:17.** As many that vowed I shall fail in life, shall not succeed but experience disappointments in the name of Jesus.

Divine carpenters of heaven break open every locked doors, every locked windows, every locked gates fashioned against my virtues and destiny, in the name of Jesus. For it is written, **"I will go before thee, and make thy crooked place straight: I will break in pieces the gates of brass, and cut in sunder the bars of iron"** **Isaiah 45:2.** Holy Ghost pull down every evil kingdom, every evil bank and every strong room harbouring my blessings. Holy Ghost lift up and dash into pieces every witchcraft embargo standing against my progress and advances in life.

O Lord speak word of favour, word of breakthrough and word of abundance and success into my life. Wherever my virtues are kept, in the ocean, in the rock, on trees, in the grave or any dark place be released unto me now without delay, in the name of Jesus. My success shall explode while favour of God shall locate me. Before everyone, young or old, men or women, far off or near, at night or in the day, at every rung in the ladder of my life, my Lord shall raise me high and make low every mountain before me. He shall level all rough grounds and make plain rugged places.

At the end Lord, let progress and joy be my portion as it is written, **"Thou wilt show me the path of life: in thy presence is fullness of joy: at thy right hand there are pleasures for ever more". Psalm 16:11.** I thank you O Lord that this month, whether the devil like it or not my promotion and success shall be announced in the name of Jesus.

As Moses rod swallow the rod of Pharaoh's magicians so shall the power of God swallow my problems. Amen.

FINAL THANKSGIVING

I thank you Lord for the answer to my prayer and for seeing me through in this prayer. I thank you Lord for raising me out of ashes to greater height, for healing my heart and for giving me hopes. I thank you Lord for crowning me with power of excellence. Accept my thanks in Jesus name. Amen.

SEAL YOUR PRAYER

I seal my prayers with the blood of Jesus and power of the Holy Ghost. Any power assign to unseal my prayer shall fail, for it is written, **"Whoso diggeth a pit shall fall therein: and he that rolleth a stone, it will return upon him"** **Proverbs 26:27.** Also it is written, **"And the God of peace shall bruise Satan under your feet shortly". The grace of our LORD Jesus Christ be with you (me) Amen.**

Praise the Lord, Hallelujah.

YOU HAVE BATTLES TO WIN

TRY THESE BOOKS

1. COMMAND THE DAY.

Each day of the week is loaded with meanings and divine assurance. God did not create each day of the week for the fun of it. Blessings, success, gifts, resources, hopes, portfolios, duties, rights, prophecies, warnings and challenges, are loaded in each day.

Do you know the language, command or decree you can use to claim what belongs to you in each day of the week? Do you know in Christendom, Monday can be equated to one of the days of creation in Genesis chapter one? Do you know creation lasted for six days and God rested on the seventh day? What day of the week can Christian equate as the first day of the week, if we follow Christian calendar? What day can we call day seven?

This book shall give insight to these questions. It shall explain how you can command each day of the week according to creation in the book of Genesis chapter one.

Above all, you shall exercise your right and claim what is hidden in each day of the week.

Check for this in **COMMAND THE DAY.**

2. PRAYER TO REMEMBER DREAMS

A lot of people are passing through this spiritual epidemic on a daily basis. Their dream life is epileptic, having no ability to remember all dreams they dream, or sometimes forget everything entirely. This is nothing but spiritual havoc you need to erase from your spiritual record.

The answer to every form of spiritual blackout caused by spiritual erasers is found in, **PRAYER TO REMEMBER DREAMS.**

3. 100% CONFESSSIONS AND PROPHECIES TO LOCATE HELPERS.

This is a wonderful book on confessions and prophecies to locate helpers and helpers to locate you. It is a prayer book loaded with over two thousand (2,000) prayer points.

The book unravels how to locate unknown helpers, prayers to arrest mind of helpers and prayers for manifestation after encounter with helpers.

4. ANOINTING FOR ELEVENTH HOUR HELP.

This book tells much of what to do at injury hour called eleventh hour. When you read and use this book as prescribed fear shall vanish in your life when pursuing a project, career or contract.

5. PRAYER TO LOCATE HELPERS.

Our divine helper is God. He created us to be together and be of help to one another. In the midst of no help we lost out, ending our journey in the wilderness.

There are keys assign to open right doors of life. You need right key to locate your helpers. Enough is enough; of suffering in silence.

With this book, you shall locate your helpers while your helpers shall locate you.

6. GOLIATH AT THE GATE OF MARRIAGE

Sex violence is rampant worldwide. Rapists carry out evil intents as if nothing will happen. Innocent girls and women are molested by faceless men who refuse to keep their Libido in check. This led to widespread cry from victims of circumstances as laughter and joy is hardly found on faces of ladies in secret and in public.

Unfortunately women are involved. With tricks and false promises, innocent girls are trafficked overseas into prostitution. They caused many destinies to sink as victims could not find their bearings in the cloud they find themselves.

There are ways out of this mess and promising steps to take. This book shall give every family and readers best way to handle every matter relating to sex violence. Obtain this book.

7. SEX IN THE DREAM

Sex in the dream is causing sex havoc in families. Many marriages reap what they least bargain for as a result of sex tyrants that molest them in sleep. These sleep spouse are either called spirit husband or spirit wife. They have sex with victims and cause marriage to collapse.

Their untold hardship on victims brought about the birth of this book loaded with prayers. The book is divided into two parts. Part one gives details of causes, effects and way out of sleep harassment, while part two is loaded with right prayers and prayer points. The book shall also tell you how to recover what you lost as a result of damage done to your destiny in the sleep.

Wake up and grab this book. It is marvelous.

8. SPIRIT OF DOG

This book treats how a particular spirit called Spirit of dog that captivates lives of millions worldwide can be put to check. This spirit is a one that brings shame before you know it. It is a spirit that drains purse and cause widespread promiscuity and diseases at will.

Both young and old, believers and non-believers can be arrested by this faceless spirit which made many mad for sex. This book is marvelous as it gives details of captivities orchestrated by this spirit and how it can be silenced from operating in a life.

Lay your hands on it for good.

9. PRAYER FOR THE FRUIT OF THE WOMB

This prayer book is children magnet. By faith and believe in God Almighty, as soon as you use this book open doors to child bearing shall be yours. Amen

10. PRAYER FOR PREGNANT WOMEN.

This is a spiritual prayer book loaded with prayers of solution for pregnant women. As soon as you take in, the prayers you shall pray from day one of conception to the day of delivery are written in this book.

11. WARFARE IN THE OFFICE

It is high time you pray prayers of power must change hands in office. Use this book and liberate yourself from every form of office yoke.

12. MY MARRIAGE SHALL NOT BREAK

Marriage is corner piece of life, happiness and joy. You need to hold it tight and guide it from wicked intruders and destroyer of homes.

13. VICTORY OVER SATANIC HOUSE PART 1 & 2

Are you a tenant, bombarded left and right, front and back by wicked people around you?
With this book you shall be liberated from the hooks of the enemy.

14. DICTIONARY OF DREAMS

This is a must book for every home. It gives accurate details to about **10,000 (Ten thousand) dreams and interpretations,** written in alphabetical order for quick reference and easy digestion. The book portrays spiritual revelations with sound prophetic guidelines. It is loaded with Biblical references and violent prayers.

Ask for yours today.

15. 32 EMERGENCY TELEPHONE CALLS OF GOD.

This is a powerful package that addresses daily emergency needs of Christians. As it is known, success comes when right key is applied to situations. This is exactly what this book entails. It empowers to draw right answer from the holy seat without sweat.

What emergency do you face? Try this book and receive solution by fire.

For Further Enquiries Contact
THE AUTHOUR
EVANGELIST TELLA OLAYERI
P.O. Box 1872 Shomolu Lagos
Tel: 08023583168

FROM AUTHOR'S DESK

Authors write for others to digest, gain and broaden intellects. Your comment is therefore needed to arouse others into Christ's bosom.

I therefore implore you to comment on this on this book.

God bless.

Thanks.